French Tea

French Tea

The Pleasures
of
the Table

Carole Manchester

Photographs by
Juliette d'Assay

HEARST BOOKS
New York

It is the policy of William Morrow and Company, Inc., and its imprints and affiliates, recognizing the importance of preserving what has been written, to print the books we publish on acid-free paper, and we exert our best efforts to that end.

Library of Congress Cataloging-in-Publication Data

Manchester, Carole
    French tea : the pleasures of the table / Carole Manchester ; photographs by Juliette d'Assay.
      p.   cm.
    Includes index.
    ISBN 0-688-11355-9
    1. Tea—France.   2. Tea.   I. Title.
TX817.T3M29.   1993
394.1′5—dc20   92-45129
                                          CIP

Printed in the United States of America

First Edition

   2   3   4   5   6   7   8   9   10

Book Design by Liz Trovato

To Shunna, my constant tea companion

Acknowledgments

As at the tea hour when it's always nicer with company, the production of this book was enriched by exchanges with old and new friends. I'm grateful to everyone who gave generously of their time, invited me into their homes, and offered a good idea, an introduction, encouragement, as well as to the many people who supplied pastries, flowers, and table accessories. I wish to give special thanks to:

My agent, Gayle Benderoff, for her wonderful suggestions, ideas, and good advice from the very beginning, and my editor, Harriet Bell, for her belief in the project, attentiveness, and excellent editorial guidance.

Dr. Franca Brunetti, Sylvia Brunetti Alary, Countess Alain d'Assay, and Countess Robert d'Agrain for their hospitality, generosity, and kindness during my stay in France.

My good friends Catherine Sabino, who encouraged me to do this book, Claudie Rappenau, France Grand, and Michele Loyer.

Tamara Préaud and Catherine Monnier for opening the doors to the treasures of Sèvres.

Jacques Jumeau-Lafond at Dammann, Kitti Cha Sangmanee at Mariage Frères, and Pierre Verlet at Verlet for sharing their tea expertise.

Bruno Baert of Hôtel Ritz, Renata Benichou, Isabelle Benita, Sylvie Binet, Chloë de Bruneton, Kate de Castelbajac, Marie-Louise de Clermont-Tonnerre of Chanel, Yafa Édery, Christine Guérard at Eugénie-les-Bains, Geneviève Hebey, Patrick Hourcade, Hilton McConnico, Maud Molyneux, Cecile Pradalié, Joël Robuchon of Jamin, Philippe Ruetsch of Hôtel Meurice, Count and Countess Géraud de Sabran, Count and Countess Jean de Sabran, Marguerite de Sabran at Musée Bouilhet-Christofle, Marie-France de Saint Felix, and Hannelore Stein of Hôtel de la Mirande, for inviting us to tea.

Art domestique ancien, Au Fond de la Cour, Aux Pucerons Chineurs, Baccarat, Bernardaud, Christofle, Christian Benais, Daum, Dîners en Ville, Fanette, Hermès, La Vie de Château, Muriel Grateau, Noël, and Odiot for their beautiful table accessories; Christian Constant, Dalloyau, E. Pradier, Fauchon, Fouquet, Furet, Gérard Mulot, Jean Marc Brenet at Hôtel Meurice, Jouvaud, La Cigogne, Philippe Gobet at Jamin, and Poilâne for their delicious pastries and sweets; Marianne Robic, Moulié Savart, and Pierre Declercq for their lovely flowers.

Georgia Downard for testing the recipes and Marina Ksiezopolska for helping with translations.

Liz Trovato for her artistic contributions to this book.

The talented staff at William Morrow for their efforts in the production of this book, in particular my copy editor, Judith Sutton.

Finally, thank you to Noélie de Ferrière for getting me organized in France, to Juliette d'Assay for her photographs and for being a good trouper under sometimes trying circumstances, and to my husband, Shunna Pillay, for his constant support and excellent assistance, the perfect tea-wallah.

Contents

Introduction

Legend has it that tea was discovered by the Chinese emperor Shen Nung in the third millennium before the birth of Christ. The Divine Healer, as he was called, had learned that those who boiled their water before drinking it were less likely to fall ill. On a fateful day in 2737 B.C., while the emperor's servants were feeding a fire with branches of wild camellias and tea trees, some tea leaves fell into the boiling water—and thus the first tea was brewed. The golden liquor was given the name ch'a.

Since its beginnings, the infinitely complex and variously flavored brew has been a source of endless fascination. Hailed by the Taoists as "the elixir of mortality," it was elevated to almost mystical heights by Chinese nobles, its first champions, who drank it from exquisitely crafted porcelain bowls. Tea was held in such high esteem that in A.D. 800 it was proclaimed a royal beverage.

In that same year, Japan got its first taste of the tonic. The first tea ceremony has been traced to 1447, and through the centuries the elaborate ritual has evolved. With its captivating ensemble of delicate gestures, every measured movement mesmerizing, the Japanese tea ceremony became so revered that it earned a place in the sacred teachings of Zen Buddhist monks. The priest Okakura pronounced that "the culture of tea puts man in his proper place in the universe."

It was not until the seventeenth century that tea, "the froth of jade," with a value of twice its weight in silver, was transported to the West. The first shipments arrived packed among rich tapestries, silks, jewels, spices, and other precious commodities, via the narrow paths and mountain passes of the caravan routes, through Manchuria, Mongolia, Iran, the Muslim countries, and Russia, and by sea to western Europe.

The Dutch East India Company, having established trade with China and Japan, shipped tea to Holland in 1610, to France in 1636, and later sold it to England in 1658. Tea was at first considered a drug in France, where it was sold in pharmacies, and for quite some time it was a much-debated subject among the members of the medical profession. One physician referred to tea as "the impertinent novelty of the century," while another spoke so convincingly of its good effect on gout that he won over even the skeptics among the faculty of the college where he spoke. A third physician advised smoking tea in a pipe after moistening the leaves with a drop of brandy, and using the remaining ash to whiten the teeth.

On August 3, 1700, the *Amphitrite,* the first of six French vessels to set sail for China during the reign of Louis XIV (1643–1715), returned with tea among its rich cargo of silk, lacquer, and porcelain. The number of these trading vessels to China increased tenfold during the reign of Louis XV (1715–1774).

Tea became the fashionable beverage in French society toward the end of the reign of Louis XIV, when members of the upper class and intellectuals gathered in chandeliered, marble-tabled cafés to gossip, debate the issues of the day, and drink tea. These decorous public rooms were more like salons than cafés as we know them today. Tea drinking was confined within these elite circles and would remain so until the end of the nineteenth century.

Not all the habitués of the salons of Paris approved of tea drinking. The brew was discussed as much as it was consumed. The famous letter writer Mme de Sévigné wrote in 1680 that Mme de la Sablière added milk to her tea—the first documented reference to anyone taking tea with milk in Europe. Later, she wrote that the princess of Tarente took twelve cups of tea daily, and that Monsieur le Landgrave once drank forty: "He was dying and this resuscitated him visibly."

Princess of Palatine remarked in 1706 that tea could make one chaste and therefore was better for Catholic priests than for Protestant ministers. In 1714, she observed that Chinese tea had become just as much the fashion in France as chocolate was in Spain.

Intellectuals as well as the leaders of society were devotees of the golden liquid. Pierre Daniel Huet, Bishop of Avranches, chronicled the ennobling qualities of the beverage in a Latin poem of fifty-eight stanzas. Pierre Petit bettered the number with five hundred and sixty stanzas, titled "Thea Sinensis." The dramatists Paul Scarron and Jean Racine were enthusiasts, as Honoré de Balzac would be later. He associated tea drinking with elegant life and put tea in the hands of the refined characters in his novels.

Balzac, in fact, possessed a small cache of extremely expensive tea, which he so valued for its history that he served it only on rare occasions, and then only to his special friends. As the legend of this tea goes, beautiful, singing young virgins picked the tender

leaves at early dawn and, still singing, carried them to the emperor. An imperial gift of the tea was sent from the Chinese court to the Russian tsar, and Balzac obtained some through a well-known Russian minister. There was also a curse associated with the tea, which perhaps grew out of the tale that blood had been shed to protect the imperial gift from thieves who had made a murderous assault on the caravan carrying the precious cargo. Potential drinkers were forewarned that to take more than one cup of the golden liquid was an abomination and would cost the drinker his eyesight. Laurent-Jan, one of Balzac's closest friends, never drank it without first observing, "Once again I risk an eye, but it's worth it."

French writers romanticized the tea hour in their books. Children were introduced to tea in the countess de Ségur's *The Misadventures of Sophie,* Balzac introduced tea into the social life of his characters in his *Lost Illusions* and *Cousin Bette,* and, of course, Proust reminisced eloquently about tea in *Swann's Way.*

Artists including Chardin, Boucher, Barthélemy, Baschet, and Tenré painted teapots into rich still-life works and portrayed society at festive teas set in exquisitely furnished rooms. They captured voluptuous women taking tea in the intimacy of their boudoirs, or languishing at tea tables resplendent with silver and lace, and even placed doll-like children at grown-up tea tables, hair beribboned, clasping teacups with chubby hands.

One of the particularly ambitious tea paintings was Barthélemy's *Le Thé à l'Anglais,* which he painted in 1776. This elaborate work depicts a young Mozart at the harpsichord performing for the gentry seated at tea tables in the Paris salon of the prince de Conti. At about the time this scene was painted, the French aristocracy, disillusioned with their monarchy, looked to England's parliamentary system for ideas on governing. This Anglomania of the aristocracy seeking the good life extended to other aspects of upper-class English life, including an attraction to their freedom, sporty style of dress, and even their habit of taking tea.

Serving tea in France was a costly affair. Still a scarce commodity, the tea itself was expensive, and the rarefied circles in which it was served demanded no less than silver and fine porcelain for its proper presentation. Vincennes-Sèvres designed exquisite tableware for those who could afford it. Masterfully crafted tea sets were painted in dark blue, turquoise, yellow, apple-green, and in rose-pink—called *rose Pompadour,* after Madame de Pompadour, who was Sèvres' most important patron.

As late as 1830, however, there were still lingering doubts about the risks of drinking tea. A. F. Aulagnier cautioned in his dictionary of *Native and Exotic Food Substances* that its excessive use, particularly by those with delicate temperaments, would result in stomach pains, nervousness, insomnia, vertigo, and convulsions. Further, he warned, tea should be forbidden to infants and young people, as it might alter their digestive systems. He advised that a medical consultation should take place before drinking the brew, which he described as having a bitter taste but a sweet, agreeable odor of new hay and violets. The upper class continued drinking tea, and the new middle class and the provincial aristocracy experimented with it, but tea drinking became popular in France only at the end of the nineteenth century, with the birth of the tea salon.

Once launched in Paris, the *salon de thé* flourished. Its popularity then spread to the world of casinos, spas, and the grand seaside hotels in Biarritz and Cabourg. There, afternoon teas were served on cool, breezy verandas, in luxuriously furnished rooms with sea views, and at tea dances. Many of these establishments, such as Angelina and Ladurée in Paris, still exist, sedate, grand, preserved in time.

Tea consumption in France continued to enjoy a modest growth over the ensuing years, but its popularity escalated dramatically in the 1970s. Credit for this development is in large part due to enterprising tea merchants who searched out and imported an impressive variety of high-quality teas, the *grands seigneurs,* the best of the classical teas from the gardens of Asia. They selected prestigious teas from China such as the subtly perfumed, white Yin Zhen, so called because of its silver-tipped leaves; the flowery-bouqueted green Dong Yang Dong Bai; and black Lapsang Souchong Imperial, the best of the smoked teas. From Formosa, the prized oolongs, Oolong Imperial and Grand Oolong Fancy, were selected. From the Darjeeling hills in India they brought such esteemed black teas as Castleton, Badamtam, and Queen Victoria, and from Ceylon, the intensely aromatic black Saint James and stimulating Orange Pekoe Uva. The list goes on, with fine teas from such disparate places as Bhutan, Burma, Nepal, Russia, Turkey, and Iran. These same purveyors also developed variations on the theme, creating heady blends of smoked and perfumed teas, imaginative combinations that enticed and seduced a new clientele who became true enthusiasts. In France today, there is a tea for every mood, a tea for every hour of the day. Modern tearooms thrive, projecting an informal, often innovative, ambiance, and attracting new and younger patrons.

But what makes French tea unique is its accompanying *pâtisserie.* This French art form, which was well established by the end of the seventeenth century, reached extravagant heights in the days of Carême [1783–1833], a *pâtissier* who became the most celebrated chef in France in the nineteenth century. He declared pastry to be one of the noblest branches of architecture and published two books on the subject in 1815, *Le Pâtissier Royal Parisien* and *Le Pâtissier Pittoresque,* which featured his elaborate confections as architectural creations. Carême's sugary temples, pavilions, cascades, ruins, and windmills were the centerpieces of grand dinners. Carême's artistry set the standards for French pastry.

Since then, other French pastry chefs have amassed an impressive legacy and artisans today continue to create exquisite *pâtisseries,* those pretty sweets with enticing names— *mille-feuille, tarte Tatin,* Charlotte, Saint-Honoré, Opéra, Pyramide, Vacherin, Fleur de Chine . . . a *gâteau* of this, a *tarte* of that, one sweet *caramélisée,* another *meringuée.* On the lighter side, there is the choice of a buttery croissant, *pain au chocolat,* or brioche, or "le muffin" and "le toast," accompanied by a fruit confiture. Taking tea in France is a fanciful celebration.

Salons de Thé

Tea Salons

"...her expression grew serious, worried, petulant because she was afraid of missing the flower show, or merely of not being in time for tea, with muffins and toast, at the Rue Royale tearooms, where she believed that regular attendance was indispensable in order to set the seal upon a woman's certificate of elegance...."

Swann in Love, *Marcel Proust*

The golden age of the tea salon culminated in architecturally elaborate rooms of cream-colored boiserie, ornate mirrors, frescoed ceilings, crystal chandeliers, and marbled tables. They were splendid settings for the beau monde, who arrived in their carriages for "le five o'clock." Here, in a swirl of gay chatter, amid a spectacle of fancy pastries and a proliferation of teapots, the tea hour was celebrated. Children, taken along as a special treat, delighted in these grown-up rooms too, thrilled by the assortment of pretty cakes and the rich hot chocolate, for the judicious French have never believed that tea is suitable for children.

Although spread across the cities, spas, and seaside resorts of France, these graceful institutions were especially numerous in Paris. The tea salon had its start in 1900, when the Neal brothers first served tea and biscuits at two tables in their stationery shop on the Rue de Rivoli. That shop was later to become W. H. Smith & Sons, a fine British bookshop with an upstairs tearoom. Three

Angelina

years later, in 1903, Rumpelmayer opened its doors at 226 Rue de Rivoli. This posh *salon de thé* quickly became a favorite among the fashionable and was frequented by such luminaries as Marcel Proust and Coco Chanel. Its founder, Antoine Rumpelmayer, an Austrian with superb taste in food and a talent for the art of presentation, had opened his first *salon de thé* in Nice in 1870. It became so popular with the elite vacationing there that he soon opened two more salons, in the resorts of Menton and Aix-les-Bains, to cater to this select clientele. In Paris, Rumpelmayer was renamed Angelina and, nearly a century later, continues to be a popular tea salon. Although a little faded now, its whimsical, Old World ambiance is enhanced by seaside frescoes, marbled tables, and leather armchairs.

La Grande Cascade

Other tea salons, too, have stood the test of time. Ladurée, situated among the elegant boutiques on the Rue Royale on the Right Bank, suits to a T the ladies-who-shop. This always-crowded little gem, with its Louis XVI boiserie, frescoed cherubs, and black marble tables, is best known for its superb chocolate and coffee macaroons. Aux Délices de Scott, dating from 1904, is located in the quiet 17th arrondissement. Its sedate, mirrored room, with a chandelier high above, is still a haven for genteel, older patrons. Sweet favorites here are the excellent caramelized pear tart, Opéra, and macaroons. La Grande Cascade, nestled in the Bois de Boulogne, is another opulent *salon de thé* of the past. Although not precisely a tearoom, this Belle Époque restaurant in the lush park honors the tea hour from 3:30 to 5:00 P.M. every day.

Since the 1970s, more and more tearooms have opened. Today *salons de thé* thrive, especially in Paris, having evolved from strictly tea salons to casual places where *les collations* (light meals) as well as traditional teas are served. With catchy names and seductive interiors, there is a tea salon to suit any mood.

In the English style, The Tea Caddy, a dimly lit, beamed-ceiling tearoom near Notre-Dame, serves bacon and eggs and *les muffins à la cannelle* (cinnamon) while La Fourmi Ailée, a cozy bookshop-tea salon, concocts light egg dishes and offers sumptuous buns, scones, and an excellent assortment of Dammann teas.

Another in this genre is Les Arcenaulx in Marseilles, a bookshop-tea salon situated in a pretty courtyard near the old harbor. Its menu even lists desserts with literary allusions, such as "Docteur Jekyll et Mister Hyde," a dish of mint sorbet, lemon sorbet, and fresh kiwi soaked in gin. "Madame Bovary" is a green apple sorbet with Calvados and pepper, and "Anna Karenine," a lemon sorbet with vodka. The French are avid readers, as evidenced by the number of crowded bookshops throughout France, so a tearoom in a bookshop is an especially suitable mix.

Ladurée

Les Deux Abeilles

Back in Paris, Les Deux Abeilles, a cheery, flower-papered *salon de thé* in the 7th arrondissement, is chock-full at lunchtime, frequented by a business crowd from a nearby television station and models from a couture house across the Pont-de-l'Alma. Specialties of the day are added to an already long list of salads and salty—meaning savory—tarts. A bounteous display of just-baked cakes and other sweets catches the eye on entering. In another part of the 7th arrondissement, not far from where the Rue du Bac crosses Boulevard Saint-Germain, nestled between prestigious antique shops, is Les Nuits des Thés, an ethereal tearoom lacquered in ivory and blush. It is a favorite lunch spot of public relations representatives when entertaining fashion journalists, and of the antiquarians from the neighboring shops. Tasty light lunches are followed by a creamy *tarte au fromage blanc caramélisée* and other delicious desserts.

Cador

The elegant Cador, a mirrored jewel in eighteenth-century decor, sits in the shadow of the magnificent Louvre, tempting the passersby with the prettiest display of mini-pastries.

For a spiritual tea, Toraya, a serene Japanese tea salon near the Place de la Concorde, has an ambience in keeping with the philosphical concept in which everyday tasks are elevated to a spiritual plane of dignity and beauty. Its menu lists traditional Japanese lunches and creative, artful desserts.

Paris is full of *passages* always worth exploring. These bustling, narrow nineteenth-century passageways often reward the curious with a unique shop, and sometimes a worthwhile tea salon. Tucked in the Passage Rohan in the 6th arrondissement, À la Cour de Rohan is a homey tearoom with printed tablecloths and cupboards full of

A Priori Thé

mismatched Limoges. Especially good choices here are the chocolate cake, fruit tarts, and any one of the many teas described at length on the menu.

In the Passage Dauphine is the cozy L'Heure Gourmande. Not far from the Odéon cinemas and many publishing houses, it is where movie fans while away the time before the next film and book editors quietly browse through manuscripts. A tangy *tarte au citron meringuée* or a *clafoutis* would go well here with the special teas such as Morawaka, a flowery Ceylon tea, and Tsar Alexandre, a citrus-scented, lightly smoked tea.

A Priori Thé is housed under glass in the Galerie Vivienne, a nineteenth-century arcade with a glass roof supported by carved woodwork of garlands and goddesses. With the sun filtering down on the tables, it's an idyllic place to sit while lunching on imaginative salads, soufflés, tempting desserts, and a good selection of teas.

Restaurants, Cafés, and Pâtisseries

As *salons de thé* have become places to enjoy lunch, many restaurants, cafés, and bakeries have taken to accommodating patrons during the tea hour. These establishments identify themselves with signs that read "restaurant-salon de thé" or "pâtisserie-salon de thé," inviting patrons to sit down to a pot of tea and a pastry.

One such place, La Muscade, has the advantage of being located in the symmetrical arcades surrounding the courtyard of the historic Palais-Royal. In good weather, this restaurant extends outside under a green-and-white-striped awning, providing a front-row view of the goings-on in the stately park. Served with a pot of tea is a selection of delicious pastries, including a Polka, a tart consisting of almond cream and red currants, and various tarts featuring seasonal fruit.

La Muscade

Je Thé . . . me

Café Beaubourg

Je Thé...me, occupying an antiquated specialty food shop with wood interior and tiled floors dating from the early 1900s, is a cozy restaurant in the 15th arrondissement, but to many of its customers, who come for the pastries and other desserts, it is a tearoom. On Saturdays, M. Larsonneur makes sure to have a good supply of his wife's freshly made chocolate cakes for these patrons.

The historic Le Café des Deux Magots serves a special house blend, "le Thé des Deux Magots." That, along with a basket of croissants, butter, and jam, satisfies a breakfast crowd browsing through the morning newspapers affixed to wooden rods. Those seated at tables outside bask in the sun and watch the passersby on the busy Boulevard Saint-Germain.

Café Beaubourg, a sleek, postmodern café adjacent to the Georges Pompidou Center, is frequented by tourists and modern art lovers.

In some pâtisseries, a few small tables are set aside so pastries of the day can be sampled. In country towns and villages, especially on market days, such bakeries are bustling. In Provence, busy shoppers with brimming market baskets take time for tea, *fougasse* (a flat, crusty Provençal bread), and a chance to gossip with friends. In Paris, Pradier, a small pâtisserie on the Rue de Bourgogne, has a few small tables off to the side of the bakery counter where patrons enjoy the bakery's excellent *tarte au citron.* Christian Constant, a chocolatier known for his fine chocolate tarts and cakes, has made room in his shop on the Rue du Bac for a pleasant *salon de thé,* where sandwiches and an impressive array of desserts are served.

Le Café des Deux Magots

Tea Shops

A number of excellent tea shops sell their own fine blends of teas, along with teapots, accessories, and tasty light lunches and pastries to accompany tea. Sometimes there will be a *salon de thé* on the premises. Two particularly historic ones in Paris are Mariage Frères, founded in 1854, and Verlet, founded in 1880. Mariage Frères stocks four-hundred and fifty blends of tea and runs two tearooms. One is in the original shop in the Marais, the other near Saint-Germain-des-Prés. After shopping at the well-stocked tea counters, browsing among the tea accoutrements and provisions, and perhaps visiting the museum upstairs in the shop in the Marais, shoppers are lured by the strong scent of tea to the *salon de thé.* Desserts made with tea include Charlotte d'un Jardin de Thé, flavored with Casablanca tea and chocolate; Nostalgie de Marco Polo, *crème brûlée* flavored with Marco Polo tea; or scones accompanied with *gelées extra de thé,* tea-flavored jellies. There is a choice of classic, fantasy, or perfumed teas, all prepared with filtered water, infused the correct length of time, and served at the proper temperature in insulated pots. Tea is a religion here.

Verlet, which carries forty excellent teas along with coffee, dried fruits, and jams, is located in a wood-paneled shop saturated with the aroma of tea and coffee. M. Verlet is usually on hand to help choose teas, and it is wise to follow the advice of this learned tea merchant. His clientele includes many journalists and professionals from the art and theater worlds, since Verlet is situated near the newspaper offices of *Canard Chiné,* as well as the Louvre and the Comédie-Française. Seated at tiny wooden tables among sacks of coffee beans and tins of teas, the regulars lunch on *croque-monsieur* and Viennese pastries.

Mariage Frères

Liste des Thés

Glossary of Teas

boîte à thé (f.)—tea caddy

crémier (m.)—creamer

collation (f.)—light meal

feuilles de thé (f.)—tea leaves

goûter (m.)—snack, afternoon tea

infusion (f.)—herb tea

la pause thé (f.)—the tea break

l'heure du thé (f.)—the tea hour

passe-thé (m.)—tea strainer

petite cuiller (f.)—teaspoon

petit déjeuner (m.)—breakfast

pince à sucre (f.)—sugar tongs

prendre le thé—to take tea

sachet de thé (m.)—teabag

service à thé (m.)—tea service

sous-tasse (f.)—saucer

sucrier (m.)—sugar bowl

tasse à thé (f.)—teacup

thé (m.)—tea

thé glacé (m.)—iced tea

thé parfumé (m.)—flavored tea

thé complet (m.)—tea served with bread or pastry, jam, and butter

théire (f.)—teapot

tilleul (m.)—an infusion of lime blossoms (from the linden tree)

tisane (f.)—herb tea

verveine (f.)—verbena

Verlet

Mariage Frères

The Grand Hotels

Hôtel Meurice

Hôtel Ritz

In France, as in many countries, the grand hotels with their opulent settings and silver service bow to the tea hour. In Paris, the luxurious Salon Pompadour, an eighteenth-century room in the Hôtel Meurice on the Rue de Rivoli, dazzles with its crystal chandeliers, Louis XV almond-tinted wood-paneled walls embellished with gilded garlands, and Mme de Pompadour presiding in portraiture over the patrons. Classic teas and *pâtisserie* are prepared on the premises for afternoon tea.

A poolside tea is a welcome indulgence for health club guests in the swank Ritz on the Place Vendôme. In warm weather, tea is served in the respective hotel gardens at the Ritz and the Crillon on the Place de la Concorde.

Sea views accompany tea at the deluxe Hôtel du Palais in Biarritz and the Pullman Grand Hôtel in Cabourg, where Proust vacationed. As would be expected in these posh hotels, impeccable service and grand teas in the English tradition are de rigueur.

Exotic Locales

La Mosquée, an Arab mosque built in Paris in 1926, near the Jardin des Plantes, houses a Turkish bath, a bazaar, a North African food market, and a mosaic-bedecked, wood-carved tearoom. Glasses of mint tea and Moroccan pastries are served on brass tables in this timeworn Near Eastern setting. On warm days, its shady courtyard is an oasis in which to while away the tea hour.

La Pagode in the 7th arrondissement, a short stride from the Rodin Museum and les Invalides, is, surprisingly, a cinema. Originally built by a department store magnate for his whimsical wife, who liked to dress as Chinese royalty when entertaining guests, this unique cinema, with its tranquil Oriental garden, houses a small *salon de thé*. The garden, with willows, lily pond, and carved dragons and lions, is an inviting spot for tea and a sweet while waiting for the feature attraction to begin.

If travel requires a departure from the Gare de Lyon, allow time to enjoy a pot of tea before boarding one of the southbound trains. The ornate Le Train Bleu, a Belle Époque restaurant with magnificent carved ceilings and woodwork, has a pleasant bar furnished with leather club chairs. It is a comfortable spot to watch the cosmopolitan travelers with a bird's-eye view of the arriving and departing trains.

In cities and villages all over France, delightful tearooms lure visitors, promising charm, a cozy atmosphere, and regional specialties. In Aix-en-Provence, À la Cour de Rohan, a Provencal version of its sister salon in Paris, is a sun-filled, beamed-ceiling, rambling room on the historic Place de l'Hôtel. Tempting tarts of local berries of the season are hard to pass up.

In the Lubéron hills in Ansouis is Les Moissines, where, on a stone terrace overlooking tiled rooftops and the valley below, tea is served with *croquets aux amandes* or a *gâteau aux fruits.* On another hill nearby, Au Chocolat Chaud, in Bonnieux, a bakery specializing in moist almond cakes, has created a tea salon in its former olive-pressing cave. In Carpentras, Jouvaud, a colorful *pâtisserie,* offers tea at a few small tables in its confection-filled shop. Surrounded by local pottery and sweets, teas are served with their rich almond, chocolate, or dried fruit pastries.

In Avignon, facing the Palace of the Popes, Hôtel de la Mirande celebrates the tea hour with classical music and quality teas prepared under the discerning eye of the proprietress. In an atmosphere of easy elegance, one of the beautifully restored rooms of this former private residence is a *salon de thé,* an enchanting place to settle down to an excellent tea, *mignardises,* and music by the resident harpist. Breakfast teas are served on sunny terraces, extensions of the guest rooms, overlooking the tiled rooftops of this ancient walled city.

La Mosquée

Wherever the *salon de thé,* the clientele varies from tourists desirous of a brief stop near a museum, to shoppers seeking reenergizing with a sandwich and tea, to young people curious about a new place yet not wanting the expense of a lunch or dinner. Couples are drawn to the intimacy of a cozy tea salon. Grandparents pass on the time-honored tea tradition to their grandchildren. Essentially, a *salon de thé* is a sublime sanctuary for one who has the luxury of time to linger alone or with a friend and enjoy a well-brewed pot of tea and a fancy pastry.

Jouvaud

Hôtel de la Mirande

The Grands Seigneurs

China

CHINA BLACK TEAS

Considered afternoon and evening teas, these black teas are lighter and contain less tannin than Indian teas. With the exception of Yunnan, they are taken without milk or sugar. China teas are named according to type and taste. Three provinces that produce excellent black teas are Anhui, Fujian, and Yunnan.

Keemun teas from Anhui Province are exquisite teas, light and slightly perfumed. They are recommended as evening teas.

Lapsang Souchong from Fujian Province is a smoked tea that goes well with salty and spicy dishes. The fermented leaves are grilled on hot metal plates and then laid out on bamboo panels placed above burning fresh pine logs. This process impregnates the tea with its characteristic flavor.

Yunnan teas from Yunnan Province on the high plateaus of South China are rare teas with a rich aroma. They are stimulating and considered excellent breakfast and daytime teas. They can be taken with milk.

CHINA WHITE TEAS

These distinctive teas, which originated in Fujian Province, are produced in limited supply. White teas are ideal for summer as they are known to reduce body temperature. Yin Zhen is the most precious and prestigious white tea in the world. The "Imperial" harvesting takes place on just two days a year. An infusion of the silver-dotted, needle-like white leaves results in a clear tea with a subtle fresh bud aroma.

CHINA GREEN TEAS

Green teas are unfermented and are more refreshing than other types of tea. An excellent Chinese green tea is Dong Yang Dong Bai, from Dong Yang Province. The clear tea is taken without milk or sugar. It has a flowery bouquet and a mild taste. It's appropriate for special occasions.

India

India produces black teas noted for their exquisite, delicate bouquet and rich, full-bodied flavor. Indian teas carry the names of the gardens in which they are grown. The best known gardens are those in the areas of Darjeeling and Assam.

DARJEELING

The gardens in Darjeeling produce the most refined Indian teas. Grown on the slopes of the Himalayas, the teas have a muscatlike flavor and an exquisite bouquet. They are five o'clock teas. These teas are produced from harvests at specific times of the year and are categorized accordingly as First Flush, In-Between, Second Flush, and Autumn.

First Flush (April–May): Teas produced from the spring harvest are light and fresh with a flowery taste. Some notables are Castleton, the most esteemed of the First Flush teas; Badamtam, a grand Darjeeling recommended for tea parties; Mim, a tea to end a meal, Springside, an aromatic tea break tea; and Namring, a full-bodied morning tea that can be taken with milk.

In-Between (May–June): Teas produced at this time are less tart than those from the First Flush and not quite as full-flavored as those of the Second Flush. Singell is a pleasant afternoon tea from this harvest.

Second Flush (June–August): The biggest harvest is at this time of year. Characteristics of these high-quality teas are their attractive leaves, beautiful color, great aroma, and flavor of ripe fruit. Favored from this harvest are Namring Upper, Puttabong, Risheehat, Teesta Valley, and Nagri.

Autumn (November–December): The teas from this harvest are large-leafed, high-quality teas. Makaibari, with its round flavor, is recommended for the morning.

Assam

Two thousand gardens in northeast India on the Brahmaputra river-banks produce teas that have a spicy taste, are dark in color, and can be taken with milk. Some favorites are Numalighur, a golden-tipped daytime tea with a malted, spiced taste; Napuk, an excellent morning tea with a great aroma, and Bamonpookri, a strong break-fast tea.

Ceylon

Although Ceylon is now called Sri Lanka, the teas are still labeled "Ceylon." There are six tea-growing regions in Ceylon, each producing teas with a specific taste. Ceylon teas are full-bodied with a golden color. They are strong breakfast teas that can be taken with milk and pleasant afternoon pastries. Among respected Ceylon teas are Nuwara Eliya, an excellent afternoon tea; Saint James and Uva Highlands, aromatic, full-flavored morning teas; and High Forest, excellent for French breakfast.

Japan

Only green teas are produced in Japan. Known for their delicate, exquisite aroma and healthful properties, they are said to aid digestion and are rich in vitamin C. Gyokuro is the most precious green tea in the world. Single buds are picked by hand once a year from a garden that has been covered for three weeks with black curtains or straw shades to increase the chlorophyll and decrease the tannin content of the leaves. Matcha Uji is Gyokuro in powdered form and used in the Japanese tea ceremony. Fugi Yama is a connoisseur's green tea. Hojicha is a grilled green tea, light and excellent with meals.

Formosa

Formosa teas are semi-fermented. They are excellent with lunch or as an evening beverage.

Oolong Imperial is considered the best of the Formosa teas. It's a rare tea with a golden color, flowery scent, and subtle taste.

Tung Ting, a favorite from Formosa, is a reddish-orange tea with a mild taste.

Ti Kuan Yin is amber-colored with a delicate, flowery taste. It is thought to be good for health and to aid in digestion.

FORMOSA BLACK TEA

Tarry Souchong is a rare smoked black tea sought after by smoked tea experts. It's excellent with breakfast and brunch.

FORMOSA GREEN TEA

Gunpowder is a green tea; its leaves are rolled into small grains. A delicious, refreshing afternoon tea, it is often infused with fresh mint leaves.

Classic Blends

These blends are created by combining the best teas for a desired balance of flavor. New ones are created all the time by professionals and amateurs alike. Old favorites such as English Breakfast Tea, a blend of Ceylon and Indian teas, and Earl Grey, a blend of Oriental teas delicately scented with oil of bergamot, are among the most popular. Keemun blends well with Darjeeling for a fruity taste, or with Lapsang Souchong for an exotic, smoky flavor.

Fantasy Teas

These are unusual blends of teas with fruits, flowers, or spices added to create an endless variety of flavors.

Thé Chez Soi
Tea at Home

"*At that moment Valerie brought Steinbock a cup of tea. It was more than an attention; it was a favor. There is a whole language in the way this office is performed, and women are very well aware of it. It is a rewarding study to watch their movements, gestures, looks, the intonation and varying emphasis of their voices, when they proffer this apparently simple courtesy. From the inquiry 'Do you drink tea?' 'Will you have some tea?' 'A cup of tea?' coldly made, with the order to the nymph at the tea urn to bring it, to the dramatic poem of the odalisque walking from the tea table, cup in hand. . . .*"

Cousin Bette, *Honoré de Balzac*

As with all aspects of French life, individual style is evident, even when serving tea at home. While tea in a salon de thé offers an exhaustive variety of ambiance and fare, French tea at home excels through boundless personal style, taste, and intimacy. Although somewhat influenced by the English tradition, the unique French taste and discerning eye set a different table. The English tea is appealing in its classic presentation, while the French is more decorous, characterized by an instinctive, individual style that masterfully mixes the unexpected with fanciful results—simple settings being as pleasing as the elaborate.

A passion for color and harmony inspires one hostess to set her tea tables mimicking the colors of her rooms. The warm browns of the library suggest deep hues, naturally calling for earth-colored Barbotine plates, Indian pottery, and deep red table linen. In contrast, the soft pinks and neutrals in the salon are reflected in the ivory linen, white porcelain, and barely-there colors of the confectionery and flowers on her tea table.

A collector of Art Deco mixes silver with glass, creating an elegant table resembling an icy landscape. Another, mad about period linen and pottery of the twenties through the fifties, has amassed no less than fifty teapots and one hundred and fifty cups and saucers, which are randomly mixed at teas for twenty, served upon tables spread with a collage of layered linens.

For the designer Coco Chanel, tea et al. was delivered by the Ritz, transferred to her own vermeil, and served amid the elegant clutter of her apartment. In a château in Provence, the residents preserve an eight-century family tradition of afternoon tea with priceless old pottery in their immense kitchen clad in copper and tile.

With all the accoutrements in place, attention is drawn to the sweet side of the table, the *pâtisserie,* which sets French teas apart from all others. Picture-perfect chocolate creations, pastel cakes swagged with creamy frostings, colorful macaroons, and tarts and tartlets filled with custards and berries cover platter and plate. Sometimes sweet pastry is mixed with savory fare, and crêpes and vegetable tarts share the table with *gâteaux secs* (cookies). Classic breakfast bakery never disappoints. The scent of just-baked buttery croissants and crusty baguettes piques the appetite. Regional specialties such as *fougasse* from Provence, *kugelhopf* from Alsace, or flaky *croustade* from Gascony add rustic flavor to the menu.

The savvy tea merchants, aware of the French penchant for choice, know they cannot be compromised with a meager stock of a few well-known brands. With masterful merchandising, they have achieved shops of unrivaled selection. Tins from the classics to exotic blends extend across floor-to-ceiling shelves. Their exotic names romance the clientele—Pondichery, Roi de Siam, Genghis Khan, Grande Caravane, Jasmin Monkey King, Casablanca, Marco Polo. But despite an impressive array of choice, there are still individuals who prefer to blend their own combinations to suit personal taste. With *grands seigneurs* for purists, *thés fantaisies* for romantics, tea drinkers can match the right tea with the time of day, fare, and mood of the table.

Tea at home represents the best of France, its silver, porcelain, and pottery, its sumptuous *pâtisserie,* its fine blends of teas, and, certainly, the unique style of its people. An invitation to tea evokes visions of glazed tarts, intricate cakes, a menagerie of Barbotine amid family porcelain, and antique linen within the gaze of fresh flowers. A specially selected tea is chosen to suit the mood and to nourish a friendship at the tea hour *à la Française.*

En Plein Air: Outdoor Teas

Le Petit Déjeuner

High in the Lubéron hills in the south of France, near the ancient village of Bonnieux, the first tea of the day is brewing as the autumn sun warms the morning. Outside a small stone house, a garden table is set with antique drinking bowls and a rustic teapot from Apt, a town famous for its pottery. The sun strengthens, and drinking bowls are filled. A strong grand Yunnan tea awakens the senses. A wire basket is filled with *fougasse,* plain or studded with salty black olives and bacon. Pieces of the robust Provençal bread are broken off and dipped into the hot tea.

Picnic Tea

Outdoor food markets are a way of life in France. Rows of trestle tables and carts wind down side streets and into squares, piled with breads, cheeses, fruits, and savory and sweet delicacies. Travelers who happen on a village on market day have the good fortune of sampling regional specialties. A picnic of choice and a hot tea in a thermos permit the luxury of a flexible *fête champêtre* en route.

Thé Glacé

Iced tea, an American idea, originated on a steamy day at the St. Louis World's Fair in 1904 and has since been adopted by the French. It is a welcome relief from the sultry heat on a summer afternoon in Gascony. An orange-lemon iced tea sparkles in an early 1900s silver and crystal pitcher and deepens in color in the amber antique glasses. *Croissants aux pignons* (sweet crescents rolled in pine nuts) accompany the tea.

La Pause Thé: Tea Break

An American in Paris

At eleven o'clock in the morning, Kate de Castelbajac, an American journalist who is writing a history of makeup in the twentieth century, takes a tea break with a colleague in her salon. Surrounded by research books and photographs, her tea, a Hediard melange, steeps in American artist Cindy Sherman's amusing Limoges porcelain. The artist, best known for her photographs of herself in different guises, is featured here as Mme de Pompadour, the talented mistress of Louis XV. Today, Kate serves her guest *pain au chocolat* and caramelized *cannelles de Bordeaux* from one of her favorite *pâtissiers,* Poujauran.

Chez Chanel

Early in her career, designer Coco Chanel hosted teas in her elegantly furnished apartment above her Rue Cambon shop. Always ahead of her time, she would mix journalists and business associates with friends, a modern idea then. Tea was set on an Oriental table as her guests settled on her beige suede sofa and armchairs. Macaroons, toast, jam, honey, and *crème fraîche* were ordered from the Ritz and a Ceylon tea was poured from her vermeil teapot.

The legendary Madame Chanel was a curious, restless woman, always in motion, moving furniture and objects at whim. But she loved to lounge, too. This cream-colored satin chaise longue was found by photographer Horst for a famous photograph he took of Chanel in 1937. She always took her tea with lemon.

Kitchen Teas

A Loft Tea

In their kitchen in Paris, Cecile Pradalié, her artist husband, and two sons gather for afternoon tea. An apple tart is reheated in the oven as water comes to a boil in the copper kettle. The table is set with family faience, porcelain, and linen—plates from one favorite grandmother, a tea set from another. Baskets covered with embroidered linen hold extra serving pieces in anticipation of unexpected guests. Today Compagnie Coloniale's Chine Extra is Cecile's choice of tea.

Brewing a Perfect Pot of Tea

The experts at Mariage Frères, the Parisian tea merchants, recommend the following methods for brewing tea:

Black or semifermented tea: Put one teaspoon tea per cup into a warmed teapot. Add one cup boiling water per cup of tea. The water should have just come to a boil; overboiled water adversely affects tea leaves and flavor will be lost. Allow the tea to infuse for three to five minutes. Remove the tea leaves, stir, and pour.

Green or white tea: Put two teaspoons of tea per cup into a warmed teapot. Add one cup boiled water per cup of tea. The water should have just come to a boil; overboiled water adversely affects tea leaves and flavor will be lost. Allow green tea to infuse for one to three minutes, white tea for seven minutes, and Yin Zhen (silver tips) tea for fifteen minutes. Remove the tea leaves, stir, and pour.

Iced tea: Make an infusion of tea using four teaspoons per cup for black and semifermented tea, two-and-one-half tablespoons per cup for green or white tea. Combine with an equal amount of cold water. Pour the tea into glasses half-filled with ice cubes.

To sweeten, add sugar syrup to taste. (Sugar syrup is made from equal amounts of sugar and water heated until the sugar dissolves and then cooled.)

A Provençal Tea

High on a hill in Provence, in the kitchen at Château d'Ansouis, the de Sabran family meets for late afternoon tea. This rustic kitchen is the heart and the oldest part of the castle, and the family have gathered here for eight centuries. On this winter afternoon, with the mistral whistling against the stained glass windows, a Provençal *goûter* of local pastries warms body and soul. Earth-colored pottery holds fresh *croquets aux amandes* and sugar-dusted *oreillettes,* and a hearty *gibassier* lies on the table nearby. Darjeeling tea steeps in the marbled teapot.

Salty Teas: Savories with Tea

A Collector's Tea

A nonstop collection of teapots from the 1920s through the 1950s fills floor-to-ceiling glass shelves, and teacups, saucers, and serving plates are stacked in an ornate cupboard. Maud Molyneux, a journalist, "lives teas."

Twenty or more friends are invited for an afternoon tea of salty tarts, sweet cakes, and a variety of teas. The table is layered with antique linens accumulated on Maud's endless forays to the flea markets of Paris. Teapot after teapot, creamers, and sugar bowls cover the surface in a sea of blue-green. Maud centers his teapots on the table and surrounds them with savory tarts, *pommes grenailles,* cakes, tea biscuits, and fruit. The teacups, saucers, and plates are arranged on a separate table.

A turquoise 1950s Vallauris teapot filled with Assam tea complements a pumpkin tart. A *pain d'épice* and a zucchini tart are flanked by Maud's unique collection of tea accessories. Further on are Maud's *pommes de terre grenailles,* boiled potatoes halved and spread with salmon caviar or sour cream. There are five varieties of strong and aromatic teas—headier teas for the savories, lighter ones for the sweets. Maud especially fancies Assam and large leaf Darjeeling teas.

A Catered Affair

Yafa Édery, an artistic caterer who specializes in bite-sized food, favors salty fare over sweet with tea. She prepared tantalizing treats for an afternoon tea for architect Marie-France de Saint Félix. Each item is carefully chosen for visual appeal as well as taste.

Keeping Tea

To protect tea from its enemies—air, light, heat, and dampness—store it in a tin or an opaque ceramic pot with an airtight seal.

Mini-omelettes are rolled around thin strips of ham dabbed with mayonnaise, each topped with a mint leaf and a small shrimp and neatly tied with a blade of scallion green. Salmon crêpes rest atop a squash. Ceylon tea infused with julienned orange peel steeps in a glass teapot. Plump purple grapes, rolled in goat cheese and ground pistachios, are split in half and topped with whole pistachios.

Yafa uses a special gadget called a *girolet* to cut hard cheese into petals. Thick toast triangles made from *pain de mie* are accompanied by apple-orange jelly or *leben,* Lebanese yogurt.

Sunday Teas

For many whose weekly demands leave little time to linger over breakfast tea, enjoy brunch, or indulge in an afternoon *goûter* at home, Sundays allow for this luxury. Favorite tarts or cakes are baked at home or purchased from a neighborhood *pâtissier*. The sumptuous treats travel from shop to home packaged in beribboned boxes and fancy papers that are almost too exquisite to unwrap.

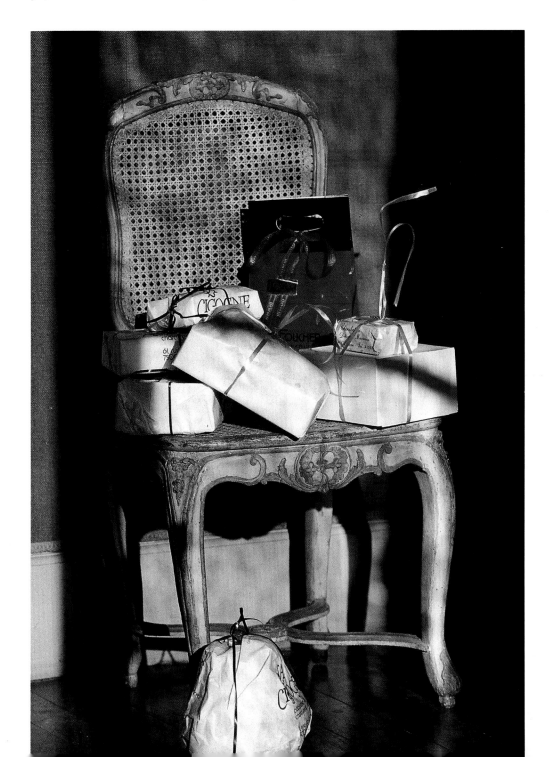

Thé à Deux

It is Sunday morning in Paris. Sunlight fills the garden of a town house and angles into the sitting room. Renata, a fashion and home furnishings designer, serves a light Sunday breakfast for two—brioche for her husband, fresh fruit for herself—a pot of Yunnan tea to share. Renata gives the same attention to an everyday meal as she would to a dinner party. Tables and trays are set with favorite pieces of her own design. She takes time for tea with her husband every day, sometime between four and seven in the afternoon, since dinner is never before nine o'clock.

Brunch Tea

After shopping at the Sundays-only organic market on Boulevard Raspail, a few friends arrive at Renata's town house for brunch. An inviting table has been set before the fire with leaf-motif linen designed by Renata and inspired by her garden. The gourds and fruit on the table mimic the still life on the wall. On this chilly October day, Renata serves smoked salmon with blinis and mustard-dill sauce, croissants, *gâteaux secs,* and smoky Lapsang Souchong tea.

A Pick-me-up Tea

Hilton McConnico, an American artist and home furnishings designer living in Paris, takes a refreshing mid-afternoon tea in the country with his favorite cookies from LeNôtre. His cheerful, Matisselike tea service brightens a gray November afternoon.

Tea in the 6th Arrondissement

At five o'clock on a brisk winter afternoon in Paris, a warming tea is set inside this cozy apartment in the smart 6th arrondissement. The fireplace is ablaze and a silver tray set for tea rests on an "X." The scent of burning wood mingles with the aroma of the warm *tarte Tatin*. A slice of this favorite upside-down apple tart is dolloped with thick *crème fraîche*, and a Ceylon Orange Pekoe is ready to pour into the china cups.

On a table nearby are a fruit-topped brioche bordelaise and a rich chocolate cake with a hint of jasmine tea, appropriately named Fleur de Chine.

Tea in the 16th Arrondissement

Chloë de Bruneton, a textile and fashion designer, possesses an endless cache of family china, silver, and linen, along with her own personal collection accumulated over the years. With these treasures and her exquisite taste, Chloë sets her tables in a variety of styles. On this autumn Sunday afternoon, tea is served in her chocolate-colored library in the chic 16th arrondissement. An antique Indian patchwork quilt is centered on a grape damask-covered table and stacked with 1900s Barbotine plates, cups, and saucers. Barbotine vases are filled with mauve roses and burgundy-tinted hydrangeas. A honey-colored *gâteau à l'orange* completes the table. An aromatic black Ceylon tea, Ratnapura, steeps in an Indian pottery teapot. Its sweet aroma complements the citrus-flavored cake.

Chloë, taking her cue from the pink, dusty rose, and gray colors of her living room, and mirroring the muted hues of her Aubusson carpet, prepares a tea table in similar colors. She layers the table with family linen of ivory lace and silver-edged napkins, adds an 1800s silver tea service, 1900s gold-rimmed porcelain cups and saucers, and *dentelé,* floral-designed serving plates, along with lush bouquets of the palest pink roses and whitest anemones.

Chloë selects a fanciful Vacherin, an assortment of cookies and confections, and a flavorful *thé parfumé* composed of black China tea, jasmine, mandarin, and vanilla for her formal tea.

A Château Tea

As late afternoon turns to dusk, the air dampens and the temperature drops. A fire is lit and tea with Alsatian pastries—*kugelhopf, bretzels sucrés,* assorted cookies, and a brioche—awaits the houseguests. With the family dog in attendance, a mixture of Keemun and Lapsang Souchong tea steeps in the teapot.

78

La Belle Époque Tea
Odette's Tea

At the turn of the century, when public tea salons were just beginning to open, and taking "le five o'clock" was gaining popularity among the bourgeoisie, Art Nouveau design was in fashion. This decorative style of the Belle Époque, which began in 1880 and ended during the First World War, was known for the flora and fauna ornamentation that was worked into pottery, glass, and silver, as well as furniture and textiles.

A tea table is set with early twentieth-century Christofle silver, stained glass, cattleyas, and cut velvet. A silver basket with a floral design is filled with translucent fruit confit, and a silver bowl brims over with sugar crystals and violet candies. A stained-glass dish holds almond, pistachio, and chocolate sweets from Fauchon.

An Enchanted Tea

In a make-believe garden, sea snails and satyrs are assembled on a bamboo and wood marquetry table. This pottery inspires a whimsical 1900s tea. The colors of the enamel-handled cutlery blend with the earth-toned turn-of-the-century Barbotine teapot, cups and saucers, and Sarreguemines serving plates. A cream-filled, caramel-topped Gâteau Saint-Honoré is an extravagant cake dating from this period. A caramel-flavored fantasy tea is poured from a conch-shaped teapot.

Art Deco Tea

Over the years, a Parisian lawyer has accumulated an important collection of Art Deco furnishings. Museum-quality paintings, furniture, and objects of the period, dating from 1918 to 1939, fill his house. A Bugatti bench stands at the entrance, a Jean Dunand lamp casts light on a Dupré-Lafon table, a Chareau table neighbors a Ruhlmann bookcase, and Puiforcat silver reflects Lalique glass.

In the salon on the first floor, on a table between a pair of cream sofas, a smart silver-service tea for two is set. A flowery Orange Pekoe is steeped in a silver pot and poured into gold-dotted Limoges porcelain. Crisp *crêpes dentelés bretonnes* and small butter cookies fill the antique silver hexagons.

When invitations are extended to elegant afternoon teas, guests know they are in for a different experience each time. Handsome white lilies grace the table laden with Puiforcat silver—tea service, cutlery, and silver-rimmed, etched glass serving plates. Lalique teacups sparkle against the silver. Geometric cakes have been delivered by Dalloyau. The Pyramide is molded in orange-flavored bittersweet chocolate and criss-crossed in white chocolate. The Opéra, a chocolate-covered square of almond cake layered with a coffee and chocolate cream, is sprinkled with gold leaf. And the Marquis, a hazelnut and chocolate rectangle, rests on chocolate shavings. These rich confections call for a grand Darjeeling, the most refined of all black teas.

The Right Teapot

If you are an avid tea drinker, then invest in several teapots—one each for nonsmoked black tea, smoked tea, flavored tea, and green tea. A ceramic teapot will take on a "lining," or absorb the oils and essence of a particular tea. A glass teapot is ideal for flavored teas as it won't retain the scent.

For mild, delicately scented teas such as Formosa Oolong, Darjeeling, or China black and green teas, use a pot with a fine, smooth interior surface, such as china, porcelain, heat-resistant glass, or enameled cast iron.

Rinse the teapot and leave it upside down to drain. Wash your teapots separately, not with other dishes because they will take on the flavors of other foods. Never dry the inside of a teapot. To keep a teapot from taking on a musty smell when not in use, put a lump of sugar in the bottom and leave the lid off.

Most important of all, never use a teapot for anything other than tea.

Tea is taken after lunch at a low Dupré-Lafon table. A tangy *tarte au citron* is served with a Ceylon tea, preferably taken without milk. Foil-wrapped chocolates offered by a mermaid radiate a golden light, illuminating the Puiforcat silver and Delvaux porcelain.

Late in the evening, tea is set out on a Chareau table. Graceful early nineteenth-century *porçelain dorée* complements Puiforcat glass from the 1920s. Squares of *pâte de fruit* and diamond-shaped *calissons* add a sweet touch. A lightly infused Darjeeling, Margaret's Hope, ends the day on a fresh note.

Glossaire de la Pâtisserie

Glossary of Pastry

amandine aux fraises—small almond pastry with strawberries

brioche (f.)—light yeast bread with a fluted base and a topknot

bûche de Noël (f.)—literally, "Yule log"; traditional log-shaped cake of chocolate

à la cannelle—with cinnamon

calissons d'Aix—almond and melon paste sweet cakes

cannelles de Bordeaux (f.)—caramelized small egg-based pastry

caramélisé(e)—caramelized

caroline au chocolat/au café (f.)—miniature chocolate/coffee éclair

charlotte aux framboises (f.)—raspberry charlotte

confiture (f.)—jam, preserves

crème fraîche—slightly sour thick cream

croissant (m.)—buttery, crescent-shaped roll

croquets aux amandes (m.)—Provençal cookies rolled in almonds

croquets aux pignons (m.)—crescent-shaped almond cookies rolled in pine nuts

fougasse (f.)—Provençal flatbread

fruits/confits (m.)—candied fruit

gâteau (m.)—cake

gâteau aux fruits confits (m.)—fruitcake

gâteau sec (m.)—cookie

gâteau Saint-Honoré (m.)—cake of caramelized cream puff pastry and cream

gibassier (m.)—Provençal flatbread

kugelhopf (m.)—yeast cake with raisins and candied fruits baked in a special mold

macaron (m.)—macaroon, cookie made with almonds, sugar, and egg whites

madeleine (f.)–small shell-shaped
  sponge cake

madeleine au miel (f.)–honey madeleine

meringué(e)–covered with meringue

mignardises (f.)–small pastries

mille-feuille (f.)–many-layered flaky
  pastry filled with cream,
  fruit, or custard

oreillette (f.)–Provençal flat cookie
  made of puff pastry and dusted
  with confectioner's sugar

pain au chocolat (f.)–flaky pastry
  with bitter chocolate center

pain d'épice (m.)–spice cake

palmier (m.)–flat palm-leaf–shaped
  cookie made of puff pastry

pâte de fruit (f.)–fruit paste

pâtisserie (f.)–pastry, pastry shop

pâtissier (m.), *pâtissière* (f.)–pastry chef

quatre-quarts/au citron (m.)–lemon
  pound cake

sablé (m.)–shortbread cookie

sablé chocolat/noix/raisins noirs–
  shortbread cookie with choc-
  olate/walnuts/dark raisins

tarte (f.)–tart

tartelette (f.)–small tart

tartelette aux fraises du bois (f.)–wild
  strawberry tartlet

tarte Tatin (f.)–caramelized apple tart

tarte au citron (f.)–lemon tart

tarte au fromage blanc caramélisée
  (f.)–caramelized soft white
  cheese tart

tartine de beurre/de confiture (f.)–slice
  of bread with butter/jam

Vacherin–cake of meringue and
  cream, often filled with ice
  cream or berries

Festive Teas

A Birthday Tea

In a château deep in the heart of the Loire valley, a birthday is celebrated at tea time. The table is set with gold-embroidered linen and family-crested china and silver. A sweet *charlotte aux framboises* is served with a raspberry sauce. Orange sticks covered with bitter-sweet chocolate are piled in a serving bowl. A Darjeeling tea, Risheehat, steeps in the pot. The mature-fruit scent of this tea complements the raspberry charlotte.

Chez Jamin

Joël Robuchon, owner and chef of Jamin, the celebrated three-star restaurant in the 16th arrondissement in Paris, improvises a tea *chez Jamin*. His *pâtissier*, Philippe Gobet, has baked an assortment of *mignardises*—miniature pastries—for this private tea party in the second-floor dining room. Tempting honey madeleines; tiny *carolines au chocolat*; powder-sugared *tartelettes aux fraises des bois; truffes au chocolat Calvados; macarons au café; gâteau aux fruits confits; sablés chocolat, noix,* and *raisins noirs; palmiers* and lemony *quatre-quarts au citron; meringues perlées; amandines aux fraises;* and petite *carolines au café* are served on gold-rimmed china. Mim, a flowery Darjeeling tea, is chosen for this decorous, sumptuous party.

As an added tea treat, M. Robuchon suggests a *crème glacée au thé vert*. The subtly flavored rich, smooth green tea ice cream is accompanied by buttery *tuiles* and Badamtam, a grand Darjeeling tea.

A Provençal Midnight Christmas Tea

In Provence, it is the custom at midnight on Christmas Eve to celebrate the occasion with thirteen desserts, the number representing Christ and his twelve disciples.

At the Hotel de la Mirande in Avignon, a seventeenth-century Provençal table is set for the *fête*. Guests can choose from an overflowing basket of fresh melon and mandarin oranges; black and white almond-studded nougat; a tray laden with figs, prunes, and dates; *fruits confits; croissants aux pignons;* almond-and-fruit-filled brioches; an assortment of walnuts, hazelnuts, and chestnuts; Noël en Provence (chocolate-dipped fruits and nuts); an almond-hazelnut cake; a quince cake; and Bûche de Noël, the traditional Christmas log.

Among the teas prepared is aromatic Noël, a blend of spices, orange zest, and vanilla. The teas are poured into silver pots and kept on burners.

Intimate Teas

French Moroccan Tea

Sylvie Binet, an imaginative stylist and writer, is attracted to the unusual. Formerly the owner of Route du Thé, a tea shop–*salon de thé*—she is an authority on the subject of tea. Her inspiration for this tea was her African table, which is laden with exotic fruits found on the rue Mouftard in Paris. Green tea is brewed with cardamom or mint, as prepared in the North African countries where the Muslim religion forbids drinking fermented beverages. Its thirst-quenching quality suits the hot climate. The brass teapot and Creil pottery teacups are from Sylvie's tea collection.

A Midnight Tea

In the quiet of the night, a cozy tea is set on a *bouti*. These reversible, highly collectible, antique bed quilts are scooped up at antique shops and used as table covers. In this intimate little room in the Hotel de la Mirande, an infusion of *tilleul* and an assortment of Provençal cookies end the evening.

A White Tea

As in a sea kingdom, Maud's intimate tea takes place on his shell-shaped *meuble de grotte*. He selects gold-edged Lude teacups, mother-of-pearl spoons, and antique Noël silk-bordered linen napkins for this romantic tea. Small meringues sprinkled with silver "pearls" and a subtle perfumed China white tea, Yin Zhen, emphasize the pale setting.

Tisanes

Infusions

Infusions of herbs and flowers have long been the beverage of sickrooms and favorite nighttime drinks. An infusion of *verveine* is thought to reduce fevers, *tilleul* to ease headaches. Their subtle flavors and soothing quality promise a peaceful night's sleep. The scent of the lemony verbena holds the essence of summer, while an infusion of the lime blossom from the linden tree, *tilleul,* perfumes the air with spring.

Tisanes Chez Eugénie-les-Bains

In the whitewashed herb room at the Maison Rose at Eugénie-les-Bains, Christine Guérard has created healthy herb teas to complement the nouvelle cuisine created by her husband, Michel. All herbs are from their own garden and meadows. Christine's favorite is lemon verbena. Whiffs of lemony scent fill the air when the hedges near their home are brushed by a pet cat or dog. The bright herb room, its whiteness warmed with touches of yellow, cheers the visitor on a cloudy day in the Landes. In a faience teapot, *verveine* steeps on an "X" by the fire.

For warm days, Mme Guérard has created a cold "tisane minceur." This iced tea is composed of dried heather flowers, corn silk, horsetail (scouring rush), bayberry, and cherry stems and flavored with lemon juice. It is embellished with fresh fruit, sweetened with honey, and served in a tulle-covered glass.

Les Recettes

The Recipes

Tarte Tatin
Upside-Down Apple Tart

6 tablespoons unsalted butter

6 McIntosh or Granny Smith
   apples, peeled, cored, and cut
   into thick slices

1 cup granulated sugar

1 teaspoon grated lemon zest

¼ cup water

1 recipe Pâte Brisée (page 105)

Crème fraîche

In a large, deep skillet, melt the butter over moderate heat. Add the apples, ½ cup of the sugar, and the lemon zest, and cook, stirring frequently, until the apples are softened. Transfer to a bowl and let cool.

In a heavy saucepan, combine the remaining ½ cup sugar and the water and cook over moderately high heat, washing down the sides of the pan with a brush dipped in cold water, until the mixture is a light caramel color. Immediately pour the caramel into a heavy 9-inch metal pie pan or round cake pan or an ovenproof skillet, tilting the pan so that the caramel coats the bottom evenly. Let cool until set.

Preheat the oven to 400°F.

Arrange a layer of apples in concentric circles over the caramel, completely covering the bottom of the pan. Then continue layering with the remaining apples. Roll out the pâte brisée and trim it to a round large enough to cover the apples. Lay the pastry over the apples, place the tart on a baking sheet, and bake in the middle of the oven for 50 minutes, or until the pastry is golden brown. Remove the pan from the oven and place over moderate heat for about 3 minutes, shaking the pan to release the apples. Invert the tart onto a platter and serve with a dollop of crème fraîche. Serves 8.

Tarte aux Pêches
Peach Custard Tart

1 recipe Pâte Brisée (page 105)
3 large eggs
3 large egg yolks
¼ cup granulated sugar
1 teaspoon vanilla extract
2 tablespoons peach liqueur

3 tablespoons peach juice
  (reserved from sliced peaches,
  see below)
1 cup heavy cream
2 cups sliced peaches
Fresh raspberries and mint leaves
  (optional)

Preheat the oven to 425°F.

Roll out the pâte brisée and fit it into a 10-inch tart pan with a removable bottom or into a 1½-inch-deep pie pan. Blind bake the shell according to the instructions below. Let cool.

Reset the oven to 375°F.

In a bowl, combine the eggs, yolks, sugar, vanilla, peach liqueur, peach juice, and cream. Whisk to blend. Arrange the peach slices in concentric circles in the cooled tart shell. Carefully pour the custard mixture over the peaches without disturbing them. Place the pan on a baking sheet. Bake in the 375°F oven for 40 to 45 minutes, or until set. Serve warm or at room temperature, garnished with raspberries and mint leaves if desired. Serves 8.

Pâte Brisée

¼ teaspoon salt

1½ cups all-purpose flour

8 tablespoons (1 stick) cold
    unsalted butter, cut into bits

4 to 6 tablespoons cold water

In a bowl, combine the flour and salt. Add the butter and blend with a fork until the mixture resembles coarse meal. Add just enough of the water to form the mixture into a ball. Wrap in plastic wrap and chill for 30 minutes.

To blind bake the pastry shell: Preheat the oven to 425°F. Roll out the dough and fit it into a 9-inch or 10-inch tart pan or pie plate, according to the recipe you are preparing. Line the shell with parchment paper or waxed paper. Fill it with dried beans or rice, and bake for 10 minutes. Remove the beans and paper, reduce the oven temperature to 375°F, and bake for 15 minutes more, or until the pastry is pale golden. Makes enough for 1 9-inch or 10-inch tart or quiche.

Tarte au Citron

Lemon Tart

FOR THE PASTRY:

1½ cups sifted all-purpose flour

⅔ cup sifted confectioner's sugar

3 tablespoons granulated sugar

2 tablespoons finely ground
blanched almonds

8 tablespoons (1 stick) cold
unsalted butter, cut into bits

1 large egg, lightly beaten

FOR THE LEMON CREAM:

¼ pound thin-skinned lemons
(2 small or 1 large lemon),
cut into thin slices and seeds
removed

1¼ cups granulated sugar

3 medium eggs

2 tablespoons cornstarch

3 tablespoons hot melted butter

Make the pastry: In a large bowl, combine the flour, both sugars, and the almonds. Add the butter and blend until the mixture resembles coarse meal. Add just enough of the beaten egg to form the mixture into a ball. Wrap in plastic wrap and chill for 30 minutes.

Preheat the oven to 325°F.

Roll out the pastry and fit it into a 9-inch tart pan with a removable bottom. Refrigerate while you make the filling.

Prepare the lemon cream: Purée the lemon slices in a food processor. Add the sugar and process to blend. Add the eggs one at a time and process until combined. Add the cornstarch and melted butter and process until well combined. Pour the filling into the tart shell and place on a baking sheet. Bake for 50 minutes, or until the filling is golden brown. Let cool, and serve. Serves 8.

Croustade aux Pommes Caramélisées
Caramelized Apple and Prune Tart

1 pound Golden Delicious or
    McIntosh apples, peeled, cored,
    and thinly sliced
¾ cup granulated sugar
¼ cup water
¼ pound pitted prunes

¼ cup Armagnac
¼ pound filo dough (about 8
    sheets), thawed if frozen
4 tablespoons unsalted butter,
    melted
Confectioner's sugar

In a saucepan, combine the apples, ½ cup of the sugar, and the water, and bring to a simmer. Cook over moderate heat, stirring occasionally, for 20 minutes, or until the mixture has thickened and most of the liquid has evaporated. Remove from the heat.

Meanwhile, in a small bowl, combine the prunes and Armagnac. Set aside to macerate for 15 minutes.

Drain the prunes, reserving the liquid, and add them to the apples. Stir to combine.

Preheat the oven to 350°F.

Butter a 10-inch tart pan with a removable bottom.

Fit 1 sheet of the filo dough into the tart pan, allowing the edges to drape over the sides. Brush the filo with some of the melted butter and sprinkle with some of the reserved Armagnac mixture. Layer 3 more filo sheets in the same manner. Transfer the apple mixture to the pan and spread it evenly over the filo. Top with the remaining filo sheets, brushing each one with butter and sprinkling with the Armagnac mixture. Trim the overhanging edges of the filo and crumble the trimmings on the top of the tart. Drizzle with the remaining melted butter and place the tart on a baking sheet. Bake for 30 minutes, then reduce the temperature to 300°F and bake for 30 minutes more, or until the filo is golden brown. Let cool slightly. Sift confectioner's sugar over the *croustade* and serve immediately. Serves 8.

Tarte aux Prunes
Plum Tart

1 recipe Pâte Brisée (page 105)

FOR THE ALMOND CREAM:
8 tablespoons (1 stick) unsalted
   butter, softened
⅓ cup granulated sugar
1 teaspoon vanilla extract
2 large eggs, lightly beaten

1 cup finely ground blanched
   almonds
2 tablespoons all-purpose flour
1½ pounds small purple plums,
   halved and pitted, or large
   purple plums, pitted and cut
   into ¼-inch-thick slices

Preheat the oven to 425°F.

Roll out the pâte brisée and fit it into a 10-inch tart pan with a removable bottom. Blind bake the shell according to the instructions on page 105. Let cool.

Reset the oven to 400°F.

Prepare the almond cream: In a large bowl, using an electric mixer, cream the butter. Gradually add the sugar, and beat until light and fluffy. Beat in the vanilla. Add the beaten eggs a little at a time, and beat until well combined. Beat in the almonds and flour until combined.

Pour the mixture into the tart shell and smooth the top. Arrange the plums, skin side down, in concentric circles over the filling. Place the tart on a baking sheet and bake for 45 minutes, or until the almond cream is golden brown. Let cool, and serve. Serves 8.

Tuiles aux Amandes
Almond Tile Cookies

8 tablespoons (1 stick) unsalted
  butter, softened
1 cup granulated sugar
4 large egg whites

¼ teaspoon almond extract
½ cup sifted all-purpose flour
⅔ cup finely ground blanched
  almonds

Preheat the oven to 425°F. Butter two baking sheets.

In a bowl, using an electric mixer, cream the butter. Gradually add the sugar and beat until light and fluffy. Add the egg whites and almond extract and beat until just combined. Sift the flour over the mixture and fold it in, then fold in the almonds.

Working in batches, drop the batter by rounded teaspoons onto the baking sheets, spacing them about 4 inches apart. With the back of a spoon, spread the batter into 3-inch rounds. Bake the cookies for 4 to 5 minutes, or until golden brown around the edges. Working quickly, loosen the cookies one at a time from the sheets with a spatula and drape them over a rolling pin. Let cool until they hold their shape, then transfer to racks to cool completely. If the cookies become too hard to curl as you work, return to the oven for a few seconds to soften. Makes about 45 to 50 cookies.

Madeleines au Miel
Honey Madeleines

3 large egg whites
1 cup sifted confectioner's sugar
½ cup all-purpose flour, sifted
⅓ cup finely ground blanched
   almonds, sifted

6 tablespoons unsalted butter,
   melted and cooled to
   lukewarm
1 tablespoon honey

Preheat the oven to 400°F. Butter two madeleine tins.

In a bowl, using an electric mixer, beat the egg whites until they hold soft peaks. Gradually add the sugar, and beat until the whites hold stiff peaks. Alternately fold in the flour and almonds in 2 or 3 additions. In a small bowl, combine the melted butter and honey. Gently fold the mixture into the whites until thoroughly incorporated. Spoon the batter into the madeleine molds, filling them about two-thirds full. Bake for 8 to 10 minutes, or until the madeleines are golden at the edges. Let cool in the pan for 5 minutes, then invert them onto a rack and let cool. Makes about 40 cookies.

Macarons au Chocolat
Chocolate Macaroons

3 large egg whites
½ cup granulated sugar
1⅓ cups confectioner's sugar
⅓ cup cocoa powder
¾ cup finely ground blanched
   almonds

FOR THE FILLING:
½ pint raspberries
¼ cup heavy cream
8 ounces bittersweet chocolate
2 tablespoons unsalted butter,
   softened
1 tablespoon eau de vie des
   framboises

Preheat the oven to 300°F. Line several baking sheets with parchment paper.

In a bowl, using an electric mixer, beat the egg whites until they hold soft peaks. Gradually add the sugar, and beat until the whites form stiff peaks.

Sift the confectioner's sugar, cocoa powder, and almonds together. Gently but thoroughly fold the almond mixture into the whites in 2 or 3 additions. Transfer the mixture to a pastry bag fitted with a decorative tip. Pipe the mixture onto the prepared baking sheets, forming 1-inch high mounds about 2 inches apart. Use a spatula to smooth the tops of the macaroons. Bake for 15 to 18 minutes, or until the tops of the macaroons are firm. Let cool completely. Remove the macaroons from the parchment paper, and store in an airtight tin for 1 week.

Prepare the filling: In a small saucepan, combine the raspberries and cream. Cook over moderate heat, stirring and mashing the berries into the cream, for 5 minutes, or until thickened. Meanwhile, in the top of a double boiler set over simmering water, melt the chocolate.

Add the butter and raspberry liqueur to the melted chocolate and stir until smooth. Add the raspberry mixture and stir until well combined. Transfer to a bowl, cover, and chill until set.

To form the cookies, using a small knife, smooth a thin layer of the chocolate filling on the bottom of a macaroon. Top with another macaroon to form a sandwich. Repeat with the remaining macaroons and filling. Transfer to airtight containers, separating each layer of cookies with waxed paper. Cover and refrigerate. Makes about 40 cookies.

Financiers
Miniature Almond Cakes

1 cup confectioner's sugar
⅔ cup finely ground blanched
   almonds

⅓ cup all-purpose flour
3 large egg whites
6 tablespoons unsalted butter

Preheat the oven to 400°F. Butter twenty-four 2-inch-long oval tartlet pans.

Sift the sugar, almonds, and flour into a bowl. Stir in the egg whites. In a small saucepan, heat the butter over moderate heat, swirling the pan, until it is golden brown. Pour the hot butter over the batter, and gently fold it in until it is just combined.

Spoon the batter into the tartlet pans, filling them two-thirds full. Arrange the pans on a baking sheet and bake for 6 to 8 minutes, or until the tops are golden. Transfer the pans to racks and cool for 5 minutes, then invert the cakes onto the racks to cool completely. Makes 20 to 24 cakes.

Croquets aux Pignons
Sweet Crescents Rolled in Pine Nuts

1¼ cups granulated sugar
2¼ cups blanched slivered
   almonds, ground to a powder

1 teaspoon ground aniseed
3 large egg whites
1½ cups toasted pine nuts

Using a mortar and pestle, pound the sugar and almonds together. Strain the mixture through a sieve into a bowl. Stir in the aniseed. Gradually work in the egg whites until well combined. The dough can also be made in a food processor: Combine the sugar, almonds, aniseed, and egg whites and process until the mixture forms a firm, smooth dough. Wrap the dough in plastic wrap and chill for at least 2 hours, or overnight.

Preheat the oven to 325°F. Butter two baking sheets.

Form the dough into crescents about 1½ inches long and ¾ inch thick. Roll the crescents in the toasted pine nuts, and place about 2 inches apart on the baking sheets. Bake for 25 to 30 minutes, or until the crescents are golden brown and dry to the touch. Transfer to racks to cool completely. Makes about 48 cookies.

Gâteau Glacé à l'Orange
Orange Cake

12 tablespoons (1½ sticks)
  unsalted butter, softened
½ cup granulated sugar
4 large eggs, lightly beaten
4 teaspoons grated orange zest
¼ cup orange-flavored liqueur
1 teaspoon vanilla extract
1⅔ cups sifted all-purpose flour

1 tablespoon baking powder

FOR THE GLAZE:
⅔ cup apricot preserves, strained
  through a sieve
1 tablespoon orange-flavored
  liqueur

Preheat the oven to 350°F. Generously butter a 9- by 5-inch loaf pan and dust it with flour, shaking out the excess.

In a bowl, using an electric mixer, cream the butter. Gradually add the sugar, and beat until light and fluffy. Add the beaten eggs a little at a time, and beat until well combined. Add the orange zest, liqueur, and vanilla and beat until combined.

Sift the flour and baking powder together, and stir into the batter. Pour the batter into the loaf pan and smooth the top. Bake for 50 minutes, or until a cake tester inserted in the center of the cake comes out clean. Let the cake cool on a rack for 5 minutes, then invert it onto the rack and let cool completely.

Prepare the glaze: In a saucepan, combine the apricot preserves and liqueur and cook over moderate heat, stirring, until thickened to the consistency of jelly. Brush the hot glaze over the cake (still upside down), and allow it to set before serving. Makes 10 servings.

Palmiers

Granulated sugar for sprinkling   *1 pound puff pastry, thawed if frozen*

Generously sprinkle a work surface with sugar. Roll the dough into a strip about 21 inches long, 6 inches wide, and ¼ inch thick. Lightly brush the dough with water. Fold over the long sides so they meet in the middle, sprinkle the dough generously with sugar, and lightly brush with water. Fold the dough lengthwise in half to form a long 4-layered strip. Wrap in plastic wrap and chill for 30 minutes.

Preheat the oven to 425°F.

Cut the dough crosswise into ½-inch-wide strips. Lay the strips cut side down on lightly moistened baking sheets about 3 inches apart. Spread open the bottom ½ inch of each strip to form an inverted **V.** Bake for 10 minutes, or until the bottoms of the cookies are caramelized. Turn over, sprinkle with sugar, and bake for 4 to 6 minutes more. Transfer to a rack and let cool. Makes about 32 cookies.

Chocolate Chestnut Torte

½ pound semisweet chocolate,
   coarsely chopped
2 cups (1 10-ounce can)
   vacuum-packed whole
   chestnuts, rinsed, drained well,
   and patted dry
8 tablespoons (1 stick) unsalted
   butter, softened
3 tablespoons dark rum

6 large eggs, separated
⅓ cup granulated sugar

FOR THE CHOCOLATE GLAZE:
½ pound semisweet chocolate,
   finely chopped
⅔ cup heavy cream

Candied chestnuts

Preheat the oven to 350°F. Grease a 9-inch springform pan. Line the bottom with waxed paper, grease the paper, and dust the pan with flour, shaking out the excess.

In the top of a double boiler, melt the chocolate over barely simmering water. Remove from the heat. In a food processor, combine the chestnuts, butter, and rum, and process until smooth. Add the chocolate and process until well combined. With the motor running, add the egg yolks one at a time, and process until combined. Transfer to a large bowl.

In a bowl, using an electric mixer, beat the egg whites until they hold soft peaks. Gradually add the sugar, and beat until the meringue holds stiff peaks. Stir one quarter of the meringue into the chocolate mixture, and then gently but thoroughly fold in the remaining meringue. Pour the batter into the pan and smooth the top. Bake for 45 to 50 minutes, or until the top is firm. The top will crack. Let cool in the pan for 5 minutes, then remove the sides of the pan and invert the torte onto a rack. Remove the bottom of the pan, reinvert the torte onto another rack, and let cool completely.

Prepare the glaze: Put the chocolate in a bowl. In a saucepan, bring the cream to a boil. Pour the cream over the chocolate and stir until smooth.

Invert the torte onto a rack set over waxed paper. Pour the hot glaze over it, smoothing the glaze with a spatula and letting it drip down the sides. Let stand for 1 to 2 hours, or until the glaze sets. Decorate the top of the torte with candied chestnuts, and serve. Makes 10 to 12 servings.

Fougasse and Olives
Flatbread with Olives

2 ¼-ounce packages active dry
   yeast
3 to 3½ cups bread flour
1 cup warm water
1 cup buckwheat flour
1 teaspoon salt
1 tablespoon olive oil

½ pound black olives, such as
   Niçoise or Kalamata, pitted
   and chopped (about 1½ cups)
1 egg beaten with 1 teaspoon
   water and a pinch of salt, for
   egg glaze

Prepare the sponge: In a bowl, combine the yeast, 1 cup of the bread flour, and ½ cup of the water and beat until combined. Cover with plastic wrap and then a dish towel and let rise in a warm place for 1 hour.

Transfer the sponge to a large bowl and add the remaining ½ cup water, the buckwheat flour, salt, olive oil, and enough of the remaining bread flour to form a soft dough. Turn the dough out onto a lightly floured surface and knead for 7 to 8 minutes, or until smooth and elastic. Transfer to an oiled bowl, turn to coat with the oil, and cover with plastic wrap and then a towel. Let rise for 1 to 1½ hours, or until doubled in bulk.

Preheat the oven to 400°F.

Turn the dough out onto a lightly floured work surface, and knead it well. Gradually knead in the olives. Divide the dough in half, and form it into 2 flat loaves. With a razor blade or the point of a sharp knife, make several slashes in the top of each loaf, pulling the dough apart at the slashes. Brush the tops of the loaves with the egg glaze, and arrange the loaves on a lightly floured baking sheet. Bake for 30 to 35 minutes, or until the tops of the loaves are golden brown and the bottoms sound hollow when tapped. Transfer to racks to cool. Makes 2 loaves.

Quiche aux Courgettes
Zucchini Quiche

1 recipe Pâte Briseé (page 105)

3 small zucchini (about ¾ pound), trimmed and cut into ¼-inch-thick slices

2 tablespoons unsalted butter

1 large garlic clove, minced

Salt and freshly ground black pepper to taste

½ cup diced seeded tomato

½ cup milk

½ cup heavy cream

3 large eggs

1 tablespoon minced fresh basil

1 tablespoon minced fresh chervil (optional)

Freshly grated nutmeg to taste

Preheat the oven to 425°.

Roll out the pâte briseé and fit it into a 9-inch tart pan with a removable bottom or a 9-inch pie plate. Blind bake the shell according to the instructions on page 105. Let cool.

Reset the oven to 375°F.

In a large saucepan of boiling salted water, blanch the zucchini for 1 minute. Drain, refresh under cold running water, drain, and pat dry.

In a large skillet, melt the butter. Add the garlic and cook over moderate heat, stirring, for 1 minute. Add the zucchini and salt and pepper to taste and cook, stirring, for 5 minutes. Arrange the zucchini and tomato in the pastry shell.

In a bowl, combine the milk, cream, eggs, herbs, nutmeg, and salt and pepper to taste, and stir until well blended. Pour the mixture over the zucchini and tomatoes, and place the quiche on a baking sheet. Bake for 45 to 50 minutes, or until puffed and golden brown. Serves 4 to 6 warm or at room temperature.

Salons de Thé

Salons de Thé in Paris

The hours of business, with some variance, are 9:00 A.M. to 7:00 P.M. Although tea is served throughout the day, the official tea hours are from 3:00 P.M. to 7:00 P.M. Some establishments are closed on Sundays or Mondays.

ANGELINA
226 Rue de Rivoli
(1st arrondissement)
Tel. 42.60.82.00

A PRIORI THÉ
35–37 Galerie Vivienne
(2nd arrondissement)
Tel. 42.97.48.75

CADOR
2 Rue de l'Amiral-de-Coligny
(1st arrondissement)
Tel. 45.08.19.18

CAFÉ BEAUBOURG
100 Rue Saint-Martin
(4th arrondissement)
Tel. 48.87.63.96

LE CAFÉ DES DEUX MAGOTS
6 Place Saint-Germain-des-Prés
(6th arrondissement)
Tel. 45.48.55.25

CHRISTIAN CONSTANT
26 Rue du Bac
(7th arrondissement)
Tel. 47.03.30.00

LA COUR DE ROHAN
59–61 Rue Saint-André-des-Arts
(6th arrondissement)
Tel. 43.25.79.67

LE CRILLON
10 Place de la Concorde
(8th arrondissement)
Tel. 42.65.24.24

DALLOYAU
2 Place Edmond Rostand
(6th arrondissement)
Tel. 43.29.31.10

AUX DÉLICES DE SCOTT
39 Avenue de Villiers
(17th arrondissement)
Tel. 47.63.71.36

LES DEUX ABEILLES
189 Rue de l'Université
(7th arrondissement)
Tel. 45.55.64.04

LA FOURMI AILÉE
8 Rue du Fouarre
(5th arrondissement)
Tel. 43.29.40.99

LA GRANDE CASCADE
Bois de Boulogne
(16th arrondissement)
Tel. 45.27.33.51

L'HEURE GOURMANDE
22 Passage Dauphine
(6th arrondissement)
Tel. 46.34.00.40

JE THÉ...ME
4 Rue d'Alleray
(15th arrondissement)
Tel. 48.42.48.30

LADURÉE
16 Rue Royale
(8th arrondissement)
Tel. 42.60.21.79

MARIAGE FRÈRES
30–32 Rue du Bourg-Tibourg
(original shop)
(4th arrondissement)
Tel. 42.72.28.11

13 Rue des Grands Augustins
(6th arrondissement)
Tel. 40.51.82.50

HÔTEL MEURICE,
LE SALON POMPADOUR
228 Rue de Rivoli
(1st arrondissement)
Tel. 42.60.38.60

LA MOSQUÉE
39 Rue Geoffroy-Saint-Hilaire
(5th arrondissement)
Tel. 43.31.18.14

LA MUSCADE
36 Rue de Montpensier
(67 Galerie de Montpensier)
(1st arrondissement)
Tel. 42.97.51.36

LES NUITS DES THÉS
22 Rue de Beaune
(7th arrondissement)
Tel. 47.03.92.07

LA PAGODE
57 bis Rue de Babylone
(7th arrondissement)
Tel. 45.56.10.67

HÔTEL RITZ
15 Place Vendôme
(1st arrondissement)
Tel. 42.60.38.30

THE TEA CADDY
14 Rue Saint-Julien-le-Pauvre
(5th arrondissement)
Tel. 43.54.15.56

TORAYA
10 Rue Saint-Florentin
(1st arrondissement)
Tel. 42.60.13.00

LE TRAIN BLEU
(Gare de Lyon, 2nd Floor)
20 Boulevard Diderot
(12th arrondissement)
Tel. 43.43.09.06

VERLET
256 Rue Saint-Honoré
(1st arrondissement)
Tel. 42.60.67.39

Salons de Thé Outside of Paris

LES ARCENAULX
25 Cours d'Estienne-d'Orves
13001 Marseille
Tel. 91.54.77.06

AU CHOCOLAT CHAUD
84480 Bonnieux
Tel. 90.75.85.52

À LA COUR DE ROHAN
10 Rue Vauvenargues
Place de l'Hôtel de Ville
13090 Aix-en-Provence
Tel. 42.96.18.15

JOUVAUD
Rue de l'Évêche
84200 Carpentras
Tel. 90.63.15.38

HÔTEL DE LA MIRANDE
4 Place de la Mirande
84000 Avignon
Tel. 90.85.93.93

LES MOISSINES
Grande Rue
84240 Ansouis
Tel 90.09.85.90

HÔTEL DU PALAIS
1 Avenue de l'Impératrice
64200 Biarritz
Tel. 59.24.09.40

PULLMAN GRAND HOTEL
Promenade Marcel-Proust
14390 Cabourg
Tel. 31.91.01.79

Source Guide

Tea Shops

Business hours are generally 9:30 A.M. to 7:00 P.M. with some variance. Most are closed Sundays, some on Mondays.

BETJEMAN AND BARTON
23 Boulevard Malesherbes
75008 Paris
Tel. 42.65.35.94

BRÛLERIE DE L'ODÉON
6 Rue Crébillon
75006 Paris
Tel. 43.26.39.32

COMPAGNIE ANGLAISE DES THÉS
11 Rue de Ponthieu
75008 Paris
Tel. 43.59.25.26

LES CONTES DE THÉ
60 Rue du Cherche-Midi
75006 Paris
Tel. 45.49.45.96

L'ÉPICERIE
51 Rue Saint-Louis-en-l'Isle
75004 Paris
Tel. 43.25.20.14

ESTRELLA
34 Rue Saint-Sulpice
75006 Paris
Tel. 46.33.16.37

FAUCHON
28 Place de la Madeleine
75008 Paris
Tel. 47.42.60.11

FOUCHER-HÉDIARD
126 Rue du Bac
75007 Paris
Tel. 45.48.68.41

HÉDIARD
21 Place de la Madeleine
75008 Paris
Tel. 42.66.44.36

HERBORISTERIE DU PALAIS-ROYAL
11 Rue des Petits-Champs
75001 Paris
Tel. 42.97.54.68
Specializes in tisanes

MAISON DES COLONIES
47 Rue Vieille-du-Temple
75004 Paris
Tel. 48.87.98.59

MARIAGE FRÈRES
30–32 Rue du Bourg-Tibourg
75004 Paris
Tel. 42.72.28.11

13 Rue des Grands Augustins
75006 Paris
Tel. 40.51.82.50

LE PALAIS DES THÉS
35 Rue de l'Abbé-Grégoire
75006 Paris
Tel. 43.21.97.97

TWININGS
76 Boulevard Haussmann
75008 Paris
Tel. 43.87.39.84

VALADE
21 Boulevard de Reuilly
75012 Paris
Tel. 43.43.39.27

VERLET
256 Rue Saint-Honoré
75001 Paris
Tel. 42.60.67.39

Pastry Shops

CHRISTIAN CONSTANT
26 Rue du Bac
75007 Paris
Tel. 47.03.30.00
Tables for tea

LA CIGOGNE
61 Rue de l'Arcade
75008 Paris
Tel. 43.87.39.16
Alsatian pastries

DALLOYAU
101 Rue du Faubourg-Saint-Honoré
75008 Paris
Tel. 43.59.18.10

2 Place Edmond-Rostand
75006 Paris
Tel. 43.29.31.10
Tables for tea (at both places)

LENÔTRE
49 Avenue Victor-Hugo
75016 Paris
Tel. 45.01.71.71

MILLET
103 Rue Saint-Dominique
75007 Paris
Tel. 45.51.49.80

LE MOULIN DE LA VIERGE
105 Rue Vercingétorix
75014 Paris
Tel. 45.43.09.84

GÉRARD MULOT
76 Rue de Seine
75006 Paris
Tel. 43.26.85.77

PELTIER
66 Rue de Sèvres
75006 Paris
Tel. 47.83.66.12

POILÂNE
8 Rue du Cherche-Midi
75006 Paris
Tel. 45.48.42.59

49 Boulevard de Grenelle
75017 Paris
Tel. 45.79.11.49

POUJAURAN
20 Rue Jean-Nicot
75007 Paris
Tel. 47.05.80.88

PRADIER
32 Rue de Bourgogne
75007 Paris
Tel. 45.51.72.37
Tables for tea

VIELLE FRANCE
14 Rue de Buci
75006 Paris
Tel. 43.26.55.13

Jams and Honey

LA BONBONNIÈRE DE LA TRINITÉ
4 Place d'Estienne-d'Orves
75009 Paris
Tel. 48.74.23.38

FAGUAIS
30 Rue La Trémoille
75008 Paris
Tel. 47.20.80.91

FAUCHON
26 Place de la Madeleine
75008 Paris
Tel. 47.42.60.11
Good cafeteria for tea

FURET
63 Rue de Chabrol
75010 Paris
Tel. 47.70.48.34

HÉDIARD
21 Place de la Madeleine
75008 Paris
Tel. 42.66.44.36

A LA MÈRE DE FAMILLE
35 Rue du Faubourg-Montmartre
75009 Paris
Tel. 47.70.83.69

LA PETITE MARQUISE
3 Place Victor-Hugo
75016 Paris
Tel. 45.00.77.36

Chocolates and Bonbons

BOISSIER
184 Avenue Victor-Hugo
75016 Paris
Tel. 45.04.24.43

46 Avenue Marceau
75008 Paris
Tel. 47.20.31.31

CHRISTIAN CONSTANT
26 Rue du Bac
75007 Paris
Tel. 47.03.30.00

37 Rue d'Assas
75006 Paris
Tel. 45.48.45.51

CONFISERIE LES BONBONS
6 Rue Bréa
75006 Paris
Tel. 43.26.21.15

DALLOYAU
101 Rue Faubourg Saint-Honoré
75008 Paris
Tel. 43.59.18.10

2 Place Edmond-Rostand
75006 Paris
Tel. 43.29.31.10

DEBAUVE ET GALLAIS
30 Rue des Saints-Pères
75007 Paris
Tel. 45.48.54.67

DUC DE PRASLIN
44 Avenue Montaigne
75008 Paris
Tel. 47.20.99.63

FAUCHON
26 Place de la Madeleine
75008 Paris
Tel. 47.42.60.11

FOUCHER
30 Avenue de l'Opéra
75002 Paris
Tel. 47.42.51.86

FOUQUET
22 Rue François 1er
75008 Paris
Tel. 47.23.30.36

36 Rue Lafitte
75009 Paris
Tel. 47.70.85.00

FURET
63 Rue de Chabrol
75010 Paris
Tel. 47.70.48.34

JADIS ET GOURMANDE
49 bis Avenue Franklin-Roosevelt
75008 Paris
Tel. 45.25.06.04

LENÔTRE
44 Rue d'Auteuil
75016 Paris
Tel. 45.24.52.52

LA MAISON DES BONBONS
46 Rue de Sévigné
75003 Paris
Tel. 48.87.88.62

LA MAISON DU CHOCOLAT
225 Rue Faubourg Saint-Honoré
75008 Paris
Tel. 42.27.39.44

52 Rue François 1er
75008 Paris
Tel. 47.23.38.25

LA MARQUISE DE SÉVIGNÉ
1 Place Victor-Hugo
75016 Paris
Tel. 45.00.78.14

32 Place de la Madeleine
75008 Paris
Tel. 42.65.19.47

QUIGNAUX
4 Rue du Renard
75004 Paris
Tel. 42.77.61.72

RICHARD
258 Boulevard Saint-Germain
75007 Paris
Tel. 45.55.66.00

SERVANT
30 Rue d'Auteuil
75016 Paris
Tel. 42.88.49.82

Table Accessories

ART DOMESTIQUE ANCIEN
231 Rue Saint-Honoré
75001 Paris
Tel. 40.20.94.60

BACCARAT
11 Place de la Madeleine
75008 Paris
Tel. 42.65.36.26

AU BAIN MARIE
10 Rue Boissy d'Anglas
75008 Paris
Tel. 42.66.59.74

BERNARDAUD
11 Rue Royale
75008 Paris
Tel. 47.42.82.66

DAUM
4 Rue de la Paix
75002 Paris
Tel. 42.61.25.25

DÎNERS EN VILLE
27 Rue de Varenne
75007 Paris
Tel. 42.22.78.33

DORIA
4 Rue Bourbon-le-Chateau
75006 Paris
Tel. 40.46.00.00

FANETTE
1 Rue d'Alençon
75016 Paris
Tel. 42.22.21.73

AU FOND DE LA COUR
49 Rue de Seine
75006 Paris
Tel. 43.25.81.89

GEORGE PESLE
18 Rue de l'Arcade
75008 Paris
Tel. 42.66.52.32

GIEN
39 Rue des Petits-Champs
75001 Paris
Tel. 47.03.49.92

HILTON MCCONNICO
28 Rue Madame
75006 Paris
Tel. 42.84.32.22

KITCHEN BAZAAR
11 Avenue du Maine
75015 Paris
Tel. 42.22.91.17

L'AUTRE JOUR
26 Avenue de la Bourdonnais
75007 Paris
Tel. 47.05.36.60

LA MAISON DOUCE
100 Rue de Rennes
75006 Paris
Tel. 45.48.84.10

LA MAISON DU WEEK-END
26 Rue Vavin
75006 Paris
Tel. 43.54.15.52

MICHELE ARRAGON-
L'APPARTEMENT
21 Rue Jacob
75006 Paris
Tel. 43.25.87.69

LA VIE DE CHÂTEAU
17 Rue de Valois
(157 Galerie Valois)
75001 Paris
Tel. 49.27.09.82

LALIQUE
11 Rue Royale
75008 Paris
Tel. 42.65.33.70

LE CHEMIN DE TABLE
10 Rue de Grenelle
75006 Paris
Tel. 42.22.40.21

MANUFACTURE
NATIONALE DE SÈVRES
4 Place André-Malraux
75001 Paris
Tel. 47.03.40.20

MANUFACTURE
DU PALAIS ROYALE
172 Galerie Valois
75001 Paris
Tel. 42.96.04.24

MARIE-PIERRE BOITARD
9 et 11 Place du Palais Bourbon
75007 Paris
Tel. 47.05.13.30

MÈRE GRAND
96 Rue Raynouard
75016 Paris
Tel. 45.25.80.58

MURIEL GRATEAU
132 Galerie Valois
75001 Paris
Tel. 40.20.90.30

ODIOT
7 Place de la Madeleine
75008 Paris
Tel. 42.65.00.95

PAVILLON CHRISTOFLE
9 Rue Royale
75008 Paris
Tel. 49.33.43.00

PLAISAIT
9 Place des Vosges
75004 Paris
Tel. 48.87.34.80

POINT À LA LIGNE
177 Boulevard Saint-Germain
75007 Paris
Tel. 42.22.17.72
Candles

POINT D'OMBRE
6 Place de Furstenberg
75006 Paris
Tel. 40.51.73.47

AUX PUCERONS CHINEURS
23 Rue Saint Paul
75004 Paris
Tel. 42.72.88.20

PUIFORCAT
2 Avenue Matignon
75008 Paris
Tel. 45.63.10.10

RENATA
2 Boulevard Raspail
75007 Paris
Tel. 45.48.08.58

SÉGRIÈS
13 Rue de Tournon
75006 Paris
Tel. 46.34.62.56

Table Linens

CHRISTIAN BENAIS
18 Rue Cortambert
75016 Paris
Tel. 45.03.15.55

HERVÉ BAUME
19 Rue Petite Fusterie
84000 Avignon
Tel. 90.86.37.66

JEAN FAUCON
12 Avenue de la Libération
84400 Apt
Tel. 90.74.15.31

NOËL
49 Avenue Montaigne
75008 Paris
Tel. 40.70.02.41

PORTHAULT
18 Avenue Montaigne
75008 Paris
Tel. 47.20.75.25

Bibliography

Butel, Paul. *Histoire du Thé.* Les Editions Desjonqueres. Paris, 1989.

Girard, Renaud, and Lazareff, Alexandre. *Paris Sucré.* Guides Hachette. Paris, 1991.

Jumeau-Lafond, Jacques. *Le Gôut de la Vie, Le Thé.* Editions Nathan. Paris, 1988.

Le Livre de l'Amateur de Thé. Editions Robert Laffont S.A. Paris, 1983.

Mariage Frères. *The Art of Tea.* Paris, 1988.

Ukers, William H. *The Romance of Tea.* Alfred A. Knopf. New York, 1936.

Index